D1649087

ınity Library
: SW
√ 56164

THE TRUTH OF IMMANUEL

The Second Attempt to Kill Christ

by

Joel D. Harris

RoseDog❦Books

PITTSBURGH, PENNSYLVANIA 15238

The contents of this work including, but not limited to, the accuracy of events, people, and places depicted; opinions expressed; permission to use previously published materials included; and any advice given or actions advocated are solely the responsibility of the author, who assumes all liability for said work and indemnifies the publisher against any claims stemming from publication of the work.

All Rights Reserved
Copyright © 2016 by Joel D. Harris

No part of this book may be reproduced or transmitted, downloaded, distributed, reverse engineered, or stored in or introduced into any information storage and retrieval system, in any form or by any means, including photocopying and recording, whether electronic or mechanical, now known or hereinafter invented without permission in writing from the publisher.

RoseDog Books
585 Alpha Drive
Suite 103
Pittsburgh, PA 15238
Visit our website at *www.rosedogbookstore.com*

ISBN: 978-1-4809-6791-5
eISBN: 978-1-4809-6768-7

FOR MY FIRST AND FINEST TEACHER,

MY MOM.

THANK YOU.

PREFACE

What if man's fundamental understanding and perception of his life, his world, and himself is flawed? Would not then all of his institutions of higher learning be propagating false teachings regarding his purpose, health and his wellbeing? If this is so, what then is the value of his education?

In light of these considerations of the present quality of man's understanding or possible absence of it, what has one man to offer another in terms of education?

If we are completely certain that what we *think* we *know* as a national or global community is true and correct, how then do we explain the disparity between our ideals and our reality?

For example, in a group of people discussing war, all (with few exceptions) will agree it to be an evil. Yet this same group (with few exceptions) will join in the war effort and cooperate with that which they themselves have deemed to be evil. In most cases, if questioned, these same individuals will state that they have no choice, or, that the *enemy* is a greater evil than war itself. All of this of course presupposes that man *has* the ability or wisdom to determine what indeed *is* evil, and further, the discrimination between varying levels of evil.

This ability is called into question by many examples throughout history, as an activity or belief once held to be evil or harmful is later praised as good and beneficial, case in point, the very idea of the earth being spherical was once unquestionably *known* to be false and satanic or *evil*.

For our current investigation however, let us suppose that war is indeed an *evil*.

Man has found justification for war in the name of eradicating the evil people, or the evil nation for centuries unknown. If this line of thinking is sane and sound: would it not seem probable, even highly likely that at present the evil people should all be dead, given the hundreds of millions slain in pursuit of this end?

Perhaps man does not *know* as much as he *thinks* he knows.

If a man were to take a stand *against* war, for example, this action in resistance could conceivably mutate or evolve into a lesser version of war nonetheless violent, leading to a possible conclusion which could be stated as "*resistance=violence.*"

Yet, what *is* violence? In general we think of violence to be physical in nature. Following this line of thinking it would seem at first glance that in order for violence to have happened some evidence of physical damage or harm must be present.

Perhaps it would be profitable to ask: what is the root cause of physical violence?

If physical violence is an absolute quality or reality without a cause, then we have no question to ask. This does not however appear to be the case, given the fact that one may choose to act in physical violence or to abstain from it.

In light of this line of thinking it would appear that our question is not "what is the root cause of physical violence?" But rather "what is the root cause of one's willfully choosing to act in physical violence?"

If, as suggested above, violence is brought about by resistance, then our question changes its face once again, it now becomes: What is the root cause of one's willfully choosing to resist?

Some might suggest that resistance and violence are products of human nature.

The author suggests that resistance and violence are products of human nature being pulled down by animal nature. Does this then lead us to conclude that they are correct who say: "We have no choice?" Or, does the question evolve further to "Do we have a choice between human and animal nature?" And if so, which would we choose?

Is it as simple as making this choice? If it is this simple, it would seem to make sense that by now all mankind would have chosen human nature. Given our obvious current state of perpetual violence it would appear that very few have chosen human nature, if it *is* so simple as a *choice*, which seems unlikely.

What if we were told an unbelievable story, by unquestionable authorities, and we were further instructed (by this same authority) that the penalty for non-belief is eternal damnation?

Being placed in an impossible psychic position, faced with eternal perdition as a consequence for internal non-belief, and bodily torture and possibly death for outer questioning of such supposed authorities *is* violence in its most dangerous and crippling form.

Then, what of desire?

Is resistance a product of desire?

Is violence its product?

Is desire fundamentally evil, as our churchmen suggest?

If evil desire leads to perdition, then does Divine desire lead to perfection? And further, can one *choose* that which he or she *wills* to desire?

Could it be possible for one to willfully turn away from the animal nature and its base desires? If so, then it would seem to follow that one could willfully turn toward the human nature and its higher desires. And again, if this were possible, would it not seem to lead us to the conclusion that one could willfully turn to face the Divine nature and Its Most High desires?

Perhaps Jesus counsels us to "resist not evil" because in his fully enlightened state, He could *see* that as mere ignorant animal/human natured creatures, we are not *yet* able to determine for a certainty what is or is not *evil*.

Jesus makes it clear by example that we are not to resist evil. When He is arrested, He explains to His disciples that He has the ability and power at His disposal to destroy His captors in an instant, yet He does not (Matt. 26:53).

Perhaps He was able to *see* that His captors were neither evil nor good, but only asleep in ignorance, and that to merely vanquish their physical bodies would accomplish nothing.

With these considerations in mind, we will proceed with our inquiry which is: why was the calendar reset to the year one about two thousand years ago?

And our further question being: Is the teaching given us by our popular *Christian* churches of men, the True teaching as was given by Jesus?

PART ONE

THE KILLERS AND THE STORYTELLERS

Something very great took place about two thousand years ago. So great was it that the calendar was reset to the year one.

The question is: *What* happened?

We are asked to be content with a story told us from childhood, the story conveyed in parts of a collection of books known as the New Testament.

This is a very nice story indeed.

We have heard many very nice stories, none of which have reset the calendar.

The question remains: What happened?

The story is told of a child born to a virgin, his name, we are told, is Jesus. We are also told that his name is Immanuel (meaning God with us), did this cause the calendar to be reset? The question remains.

The boy Jesus talks to people in places called Synagogues, these people are astounded by his wisdom at such a young age. Jesus grows to manhood gathers twelve men together, his close friends perhaps, the story calls them disciples. These disciples call Jesus "Master," and he talks to them and teaches them much and they are astounded.

The story continues, and woven through it is the message that Jesus is the son of God, what is more interesting he is said to be the *only* son of God.

Jesus travels far and wide preaching what is called in the story, "The Gospel," which means, we are told, "The Good News." This good news, we are told, is that by simply believing in Jesus we will be forgiven our *sins*, go to a marvelous place called Heaven, and live there forever. During these journeys Jesus also, we are told, heals the sick with the touch of his hands and performs many other wondrous things called "miracles."

This story is indeed wondrous, and if all of this is actually true then it could be supposed that this in a nutshell is the reason why the calendar was reset.

The problem with this nutshell story is that we seem to find many stories in human history of people who, we are told, did wondrous things which could be called miracles. In some of these stories the hero, we are told once again, born of a virgin, is the son of God. In some other stories, we are told, the hero is not the son of God, but God Himself.

In our nutshell story, we are told, Jesus is actually both God and son of God.

Is this why the calendar was reset?

It appears unlikely.

The question remains.

The story goes on to tell us that eventually some people called the Jews and some others called the Pharisees, grew angry with the activities of Jesus and with the things He said.

Jesus was betrayed by one of his twelve disciples, taken to jail, then to some sort of court proceeding after which he was sentenced to death. Jesus was hung on a cross, we are told, and there He died.

The story has a twist however, Jesus rose from the dead three days later, we are told, and after being witnessed by his disciples and some other people He is said to have gone through the clouds into Heaven.

It should be noted here that many such stories of the hero being raised from, or brought back from the dead are in print today, interestingly however these stories, we are told, are only *myths*.

Now another question must be asked: What exactly was it that Jesus said or did that prompted the Jews and the Pharisees to hate Him so much that they had Him put to death?

We are given an answer to this question in the New Testament books of the Bible. We are told that Jesus had to be killed in order to fulfill predictions (called "Prophecies"), which are written in another collection of books of the Bible called The Old Testament. We are further told that Jesus's death was to be a payment of some sort for all of the wrongdoing (here called *sin*) which mankind would or could do for all time.

It may astonish the reader to note that Jesus, we are told, (the innocent) had to be *sacrificed* to pay for (or atone for) the evil deeds of the guilty.

Some would call this the very definition of paganism!

Now the entire story becomes very interesting indeed, for we are told that Jesus was born a Jew, and that the Old Testament books are the books *of* the Jews. Was not Jesus one of their own?

Yet another question.

If we read the New Testament books for ourselves (without coaching or instruction from the clergy or their seminaries) we will find Jesus saying many things which clearly point to the conclusion that He was turning away from the long held laws and traditions of the Old Testament. In essence, He was turning away from being a Jew. In addition He was turning some other Jews with Him, many of them, we are told. Also, He was gathering many followers known as Gentiles, these were people who were not Jews, and that is about as much as the story tells us about them.

So perhaps we could guess that the Jews and Pharisees were concerned that Jesus was becoming too powerful, and so, out of fear that He might overthrow them, they had Him killed.

This idea of Jesus overthrowing or overpowering the Jews and Pharisees falls flat however, if we read what Jesus was teaching.

Matthew 5:39, 5:44
These and many other passages teach only kindness, love and forgiveness. Even when we are struck by another, we are instructed by Jesus to love this enemy. So what were the Jews and Pharisees in fear of?

After Jesus was put to death, we are told, His disciples carried on his message of peace and love and gained many followers. Even at this day there are countless orders, churches and religions that call themselves "Christian," said to mean "followers of Jesus the Christ."

When we visit these groups however, we find that they advocate many things far from the teaching of Jesus.

Most of these "Christian churches" approve of the killing of people for example, so long as it is done in a war which has been deemed "righteous" by the church.

I have read the teachings of Jesus Christ thoroughly, and have not found Him to approve of killing of people in war or otherwise.

Many of these "Christian churches" go so far as to send representatives known as chaplains to encourage young "Christian" men to kill other men in these wars.

It is worth noting that legislation has recently been passed in the United States of America to extend this patriotic *honor* also to include young women. Even to a child there is a clear difference between the teaching of Jesus Christ in the New Testament, and the teaching done in churches today said to be "Christian."

So what is missing?

The Truth.

Somewhere between the words in the New Testament and the reality of the teaching of the popular modern churches lies the Truth. They cannot be the same, as they clearly oppose one another.

So what *is* the Truth?

It must be this Truth which was the cause of the reset of the calendar.

THE SECOND ATTEMPT TO KILL CHRIST

In the days following the murder of Jesus, His disciples were not known as Christians, but rather as followers of *the Way*. These men passed on the teachings of their Master to many others. This activity was the beginning of a large movement within the empire of the Romans. As this movement gained in members and popularity, Roman officials became worried about losing power to a new regime.

This fear among the Romans also extended to the Jews, for they then also held much worldly power.

There was much concern due to the fact that even though they had killed the man Jesus, His followers and His message remained, and worse still, His followers gained in numbers.

This was the time when the followers of the *Way* began to be persecuted. Many were murdered by hanging on a cross, some tortured or burned at the stake, some whipped and still others were thrown to lions.

This practice of persecution went on for some years, we are told. But there was a problem, the followers of the *Way* were not losing numbers, but rather gaining. It seems that the followers of the *Way* had something which the authorities could not kill, much less understand. This power, held by the followers of the *Way* is called Faith.

It is the author's position that at about this time, a decision was made by the men of worldly power in that region, that though they had killed the *Messenger*, the *Message* of the *Way* taught by Jesus couldn't be stamped out through torture and murder.

The solution reached was to *spin* the story and the teaching in order to dilute and pervert it in order to serve their own worldly purposes. In this way, they use *Jesus* in an attempt to destroy Jesus the Christ, The Truth. This attempt is today revealing its failure, as people begin to awaken to the Truth that Jesus was a man, whose body was killed, but whose *essence* or True Christ Self lives on, and may be realized by any who desire to follow His teaching of purification and regeneration.

Now then, let us return to our discussion where we left off, with Faith.

Today if we attend a meeting or church service in what is called a "Christian" church, we are led to think that Faith is the same as believing. In fact, many sects preach that all that is needed to attain eternal life in Heaven is to say words such as: "I accept Jesus Christ as my personal savior." Some say that simply by calling on the name "Jesus," our wishes or prayers will be granted.

The reader perhaps may forgive the author as seeing this behavior as something other than Faith, perhaps a belief in magic words?

Could what has been written above be the Faith taught by the Man Jesus? If so, why was He put to death and His followers also, when today millions preach and practice this so-called *faith* without persecution, in fact, they seem to be flourishing and prospering?

The question of Truth and Faith remains.

TRUTH

Let us continue our inquiry and discussion with the question of Truth, for it seems that to begin with Faith could be an error in that we might be led into the dead end of having faith in that which we were not certain was true.

Of truth Jesus says: "And you shall know the truth and the truth shall make you free" (John 8:32).

Yet, what does Jesus say that the Truth *is*? "I am the way, the truth, and the Life. No one comes to the Father except through Me." This He says, but what real meaning does it have for us? Until we truly *know* what the Truth *is*, it means little or nothing.

Jesus says He *is* the Truth. How is this possible? Is not the Truth a principle which is absolute?

Yes, the Truth *is absolute*, and so is He! Here Jesus speaks from His Absolute Most High Christ Self, He *is* the *Truth*, and it follows that the anti-Christ *is* the *lie*. Remove the lie, and you'll *see* the Truth!

We are told by our popular churchmen that we must *believe* in the *idea* that Jesus died for our sins. The penalty for disbelief is as always, eternal hellfire. As was mentioned above, this sacrificing of the innocent to atone for the sins of the guilty is the essence of paganism. Beyond the fact of this idea being purely pagan, there is a further reason to question the validity of what we've been told by our popular churchmen for centuries. The reason is this: If we truly have Faith in the Truth of the resurrection and eternal life, as we are instructed by Jesus, then what *death* truly took place? The physical body of the mere man Jesus did perish, this is undeniable. However, if we are in the Faith in Truth, then we know without question that the True Man Jesus, did not die! The lie exposes itself!

In light of this revelation, what reason have we for shame, guilt or tears?

No reason!

We have been led down a blind alley by blind teachers for two millennia.

The Day of Truth is dawning.

In our present day courts of law, witnesses and others are required to swear an oath to: "tell the truth, the whole truth, and nothing but the truth." This action presupposes the individual taking the oath to be untrustworthy; otherwise, what would be the need of an oath? And what if the person swearing the oath *is* a liar? Now we have a liar swearing to tell the truth. What truth?

The question remains.

On this subject it is worth noting that Jesus forbids us the swearing of oaths (Matthew 5:34).

I have attended many denominations and churches all calling themselves Christian institutions. These groups have many different beliefs, views and doctrines concerning what *true* Christianity means and is. Often within these churches we find sub-groups with further differing ideas and beliefs. All of these groups do, however, seem to hold two basic beliefs in common. First, each is convinced that their doctrine is the one and only true way of Christianity. And secondly, they all agree that the Bible is the unquestionable true word of God.

Let us address the first belief first. How is it possible to have hundreds of different churches (all calling themselves Christian) with hundreds of different belief systems, all calling their own, the single truth? It seems clear that one of two conclusions could be reached, either they are all right, or, they are all wrong. Let the reader decide for him or herself.

The second belief held in common by these churches is that the Bible is the unquestionable true word of God, this belief extends further still, that the book itself is sacred.

It may interest the reader to know that at the time of Jesus and the followers of His Way, no Bible existed.

I have upon my desk at this moment two Bibles written just 69 years apart, in them I find countless differences in wording, phrasing, punctuation and capitalization of first letters of words.

Finding such variance in less than a hundred years, it boggles one's mind what changes may have been made in nearly two thousand years, plus several thousand years more in the case of the Old Testament books.

Some changes were made by mistake, some others perhaps with purpose. Those changes made by mistake must be forgiven in light of human error and imperfection, and in light of the massive task of translation and manual reproduction of ancient Hebrew and Greek texts. Of those changes done with purpose, more will be said later in this work.

Having attended many different sects of the religion today known as "Christian," the author is fully aware of the belief system which requires unquestioned belief in the teaching of the doctrine of the given church, the penalty for such questioning often being eternity spent burning in hell. I urge you to read on fearlessly, as God and Jesus Christ are not being doubted or questioned herein, rather, only what we have been told by men is put to the test, in the name of Truth.

Since the Bible is held by many to be the unquestionable truth, it follows that we must take a good honest look at this book.

A Brief History of the Bible

The Old Testament books were written, revised, edited and reedited between approximately 1,000 B.C. and 100 A.D., they were again translated by Jerome in the fourth century A.D. This translation is considered the official version of the Roman Catholic Church.

(Note: This time frame coincides with the conversion of Constantine, spoken of later in this work.)

It is thought that the Gospels of the New Testament are based on collections of sayings and acts of Jesus, current in the fifty years or so after His death.

Erasmus produced a new edition of the Greek text of the New Testament in 1516 A.D. derived from the comparison of manuscripts (SOURCE: Webster's New Dictionary and Thesaurus of the English Language).

(Note: It is worth pointing out that at this time there would be no remaining earthbound living followers of the

Way taught by Jesus, to raise questions or objections to any of the statements made in this translation.)

In this section we are attempting to view the Truth as told and known by Jesus in His time, since the overall question of this work is: What happened of such great impact which caused men to reset the calendar to the year one?

To this end we have addressed the influences of translations and reproductions of the texts in order to bring to light the possibility of this book known as The Holy Bible, perhaps not being as trustworthy and truthful as we have for centuries been led (by men) to believe it is.

In light of these considerations it is clearly important to give a brief history of the most influential church organization involved in the translation and reproduction of the book known as the Holy Bible, the Roman Catholic Church.

THE ROMAN CATHOLIC CHURCH

Constantine I "The Great" lived from (280-337 A.D.), he was the first Christian Roman Emperor (306-337 A.D.), converted to Christianity (312 A.D.) on the eve of a battle. He established toleration of Christianity throughout the Roman Empire (with the Edict of Milan 313 A.D.).

Note: This appears to the author to be the beginning of the Roman Catholic Church, and may have been the final death blow to the Truth (for a time) which was preached by Jesus, as the Holy teaching of Jesus was married to the worldly filth of politics.

In Catholic countries interpretation of the scriptures remained the province of the clergy, and was held less important than the tradition of the church.

A court of the Roman Catholic Church known as the Inquisition was set up in (1233 A.D.) to inquire into what was called the heresy of the Albigenses. This extended to any others who might disagree with or question the doctrines of the

Roman Catholic Church. It became notorious for its use of torture and secret denunciation. Many were also put to death by this court of the Roman Catholic Church.

Over a period of three to six hundred years the killing went on. Estimates vary from tens of thousands to several million butchered, exact counts are not available as they remain the secret property of the perpetrators.

It should be kept in mind that at the time of the Inquisition, the Roman Catholic Church was the supreme authority, above any governments in the area. We may further see that the earthly power of the church depended completely upon a population of absolute believers, or at the very least, people too frightened to raise any questions concerning church doctrine or authority. Those who did dare to raise questions were subjected to the devices of the Inquisition. We can only imagine the effects upon a population caused by the witnessing of such brutality as was used in the court of the Inquisition.

Parents, fearing for the very lives of their children, would raise them into a blind belief in the church.

This fear based, make believe, belief system, forced upon the population through the terrorism of the court of the Inquisition could be called a psychic virus (see Matthew 16:6 and 16:12).

This psychic virus, once firmly established, is self-perpetuating, through absolute blind belief in the authority of the church, and in the idea that one of the ways to salvation is found in recruiting new members, and through the killing of non-believers.

In this manner, the virus of the false faith spread, grew, and mutated over centuries, leaving hundreds of millions psycho-spiritually crippled and broken.

A large portion of this psycho-spiritual virus is manifested in the mentally diseased state known as cognitive dissonance, in which an individual holds two opposing beliefs in mind. In this case, thinking of oneself as a follower of the teachings of Jesus, yet obligated by a code of so called patriotism and duty, upheld by the church, calling for the killing of one's fellow man (deemed evil by the church) in wars, sanctified by the clergy.

This abject dysfunction of the will creates such inner anxiety and turmoil, that it manifests itself in a variety of mental, emotional and physical diseases. The mental and emotional diseases are often concealed with prescription medications, or through self-medication by abuse of alcohol or other drugs available. The physical diseases are most often attributed to heredity (which is in part true, in light of the psychic virus being passed from generation to generation) or to environment or defects at birth.

The symptoms of both physical and mental/emotional diseases have been treated for centuries with little, if any success.

The cause has been overlooked out of fear, brought about by the cause itself.

These people known as Catholics must however be forgiven, if we are to consider ourselves to be followers of the *Way*, as taught by Jesus. Perhaps a more logical reason for their forgiveness is found in the understanding that they were (and many still are) under the complete influence of the imposter self, called by Jesus, Satan.

The great error made by them is in attempting to rid the world of Satan *without*, in others, never realizing he dwells *within*, if permitted.

More will be said later in this work concerning this "imposter self."

Whenever as children we attempted to stand upon our spiritual legs, many of us found them broken by our spiritually crippled parents, teachers and clergy. Those who did this damage are to be forgiven, for they too were crippled by those to whom they looked for Truth. This is the age old story, when man looks to man for Truth and Light, without exception he will find only falsehood and darkness.

PURPOSEFUL CHANGES TO THE BIBLE
Comparing the Killers with the Storytellers

Earlier in this work we spoke of the evident turning away from Jewish laws and traditions openly spoken of and demonstrated by Jesus. This calls into question the reason or logic, or perhaps purpose in joining what are today known as the Old Testament books with what are known as the New Testament books. In addition, if we read the Old and New Testaments for ourselves, free of any coaching or guidance from the clergy, we will find a marked difference in character between the God spoken of in the Old Testament, and That of the New Testament. The God of the Old Testament is clearly shown (in many cases) to be angry and violent. He is also often shown to be closely involved with war in one way or another. He is portrayed in many stories as a punisher of men.

What are we to glean from this? Did the One True God change so much? Does He have a split personality?

Is the God shown us by men in the Old Testament the same God spoken of and emulated by Jesus?

The Old and New Testaments appear to be woven together based on Old Testament prophecies that appear to fit extremely well with New Testament stories. The New Testament was written many years after the Old Testament, so it follows (for a fearless mind) that it would be quite a simple task to make the two fit.

Remembering that Jesus was physically killed more than fifty years prior to the drafting of the New Testament books He would certainly not have been available to perform any proofreading or editing for accuracy within these writings. Yet we seem to be inclined to believe every word without question.

Taking into account that those who had Jesus put to death were the men of worldly power in their time, and these same men of later generations of worldly power would assemble a book for future generations to read as an accurate account of what took place, should we believe them?

After all, we believe without reservation that men of worldly power had Jesus killed, why on earth would we believe the story told us by these same men? And, what happened to the Scribes, the Pharisees and the Chief Priests who were the principal accusers and persecutors of Jesus? Did these people all give up their worldly cause after having Jesus put to death?

Perhaps they simply changed the name by which they are known. Perhaps their new names are the *sheep's clothing*, and they are indeed the *wolves*.

These questions have the hand and footprints of men with a purpose all over them. The purpose is the same one that men of worldly power have always had. This purpose is to instill fear and doubt, the dark twins of their father, the imposter. With fear and doubt firmly in place, men may be herded with ease, much like cattle. It is not sufficient for such as these to take men's possessions, land or money, they desire to possess men!

The further intent of the killers and the storytellers was to so confuse and confound those who would later read their work, that people would turn away from the seeking of Truth, or out of fear of hell's fire (provided by their work) would push on in make believe faith.

This make believe faith is based in fear and false hope, and is best illustrated in the widespread church dogma which would have us believe that Heaven may only be found in the distant future in a faraway place, reached through payments made to the church and unquestioning belief in the authority of the church, and then only after the physical body perishes.

This one example of false church dogma is clearly shown to be a lie by the words of Jesus.

"For indeed, the kingdom of God is within you" (Luke 17:21).

This one saying demonstrates how one may find the *Way* without a church or institution of man.

There is one saying of Jesus well known to most people that strikes great fear into the heart of the deceiver: "And you shall know the Truth, and the Truth shall make you free."

The deceiver thrives on bondage, Free Men, True Men, cannot be bullied, frightened or controlled like puppets. Jesus was and is a threat to the ruler of the world, for He was showing men the *Way* to Freedom in Truth, for this reason He was slain and no other.

At the time of the making of the Bible, many sayings of Jesus had become well known and in common usage by the followers of the *Way*, and others. These are the few which remain in our current Bible, however diluted some have become over time and reproduction. The reason these few remain is that the men in power knew full well that if they left out all of the Truth, their deception would be exposed, and their plot destroyed.

Fortunately for us, all that is needed of Truth is a tiny scrap, for Truth is not measured in volume or weight, but in quality alone.

Try as they might to bury the Truth in a thick book, it is now beginning to show through the cracks in their imperfect work.

In addition to this, the men of worldly power are never given to doing their own dirty work, they most often pay someone to do it for them, as they have always plenty of money since it is of their creation. This we see example of in the thirty pieces of silver paid to Judas for his contribution.

In the case of the production of the Bible those paid were scribes, and as The Divine is present in all places at all times, so It was here. Some of these scribes had knowledge far exceeding that of their employers, though they kept it concealed from them.

In this manner, a trail of crumbs, so to speak, was left for the Faithful in Truth.

FAITH

In addition to faith being confused with belief as mentioned earlier, the word *faith* has also been corrupted into the meaning of *religion*. For example, we often hear people speak of the Jewish *faith*, or the Christian *faith*, as if many flavors or varieties of Faith exist.

This confused line of thinking is woven into the story/picture through pulpit, media and popular culture, and over time has assumed the mantle of *truth*.

If we could agree that Faith in Truth may be compared to absolute *knowing*, which would be far beyond the scope of mere *belief*, perhaps we may have a glimmer of an idea of what Faith Truly *is*. With this in mind, a further question must be asked. What is the object of our Faith?

We have looked at the book called the Holy Bible. We have discussed the clear possibility of its corruption by men. We have also seen a strong motive and ample opportunity for such corruption by men.

What are we left with?

We have only the Truth.

No book, including the one you now hold in your hands, can give anyone the Absolute Truth. The most that any book or teacher can do, is to point the way *to* the Truth. Each must find his or her own way.

A Master on the other hand, such as Jesus, can do one thing more. A Master can convey a discipline which may be used as a tool box in order to find the *Way*.

The word *discipline* is a cousin of the word *disciple*, a discipline is what Jesus taught to the twelve, and what they *began* to pass on to the early followers of the *Way*.

Jesus never said: *Worship Me.*

Jesus said: "Therefore whoever hears these sayings of Mine, and *does* them, I will liken him to a wise man who built his house on the rock" (Matt. 7:24).

In the Presence of Christ

Beyond the corruption of the words printed in the Bible, there is another tool used by the deceivers. This tool is in the interpretation of the words. In many instances the words could not be corrupted, since the sayings of Jesus were well known to many in those days. People in the early days (following the tainted marriage of the Teachings with the filth of politics) were spoon fed the *politically accepted* meanings of passages, much as it is done today. And as always, the penalty for questioning the accepted interpretations of the church is eternal hell fire, also provided by the storytellers.

Jesus the man was not at physical birth the Christ. Rather, through His disciplined inner work in cooperation with the Most High, He realized in His time, His Christhood (see Luke 13:32).

We have been led astray by many churches of men to falsely believe Jesus to be the *only* Son of God. Jesus is *a*

Son in God, one of many human manifestations in God, each to come in His own time. Jesus states this clearly several times in His teachings.

"Only begotten Son," as it appears in print today, was transposed according to twelfth century scripture as reported in the writings of Meister Eckhart. The original text read, "The Son begotten only of the Father." Hence, only of the Spirit, not a birth in flesh. The only Son *is* Christ, this much is true, yet all carry within, the potential for such realization.

When Jesus spoke the words "I am the Way the Truth and the Life. Deny yourself, pick up your cross and follow Me," His meaning was not to deny ourselves of goods and righteous comforts, as we have been falsely told by our churchmen and clergy, but rather to deny our false selves, called by Jesus, "Satan."

When Jesus said, "Follow Me," His meaning is not *worship Me*, as we have been falsely taught by our indoctrinated churchmen, but rather, to follow His teachings of selflessness in order to follow in His footsteps *spiritually*, to the realization of our own Christhood, each in His own time.

The birth of Christ spoken of in the New Testament is the *spiritual* birth which took place within the man Jesus, upon His preparation of the Temple *within*. This is the inner *spiritual* meaning of the passage which puts Jesus in the Temple, casting out the money changers. It is clearly symbolic of the inner cleansing Jesus spoke of so often (Matt 21:12).

This preparation is the purification and emptying of all aspects of the false self. At the point of absolute purification, the *Temple* may be spoken of as "virgin." This is the true meaning of the *virgin birth*.

Jesus plainly tells us, "The Kingdom of God is within You," yet we are led to think and believe by blind churchmen, that the Kingdom is far away in *physical* distance and far removed from us in some imagined future time, and may only be reached after the physical body perishes.

Jesus is not telling us to follow Him through worship of Him, but rather to follow Him through Truth! This Truth may only be found within, in meeting with the Source. Each must do his or her own inner cooperative *work* in order to make the *Way* straight for the *Birth*. This spiritual Birth brings about the new Man, the True Creation, the Christ Being, perpetual and without end.

There is no cause for haste, fear, doubt or worry in this Work, and no place for guilt, for the Will of the Most High is done not in time, but rather in Truth.

The coming of the Son of Man, spoken of by Jesus has been twisted and perverted by blind teachers. These teachers tell us of the return of Jesus, yet this is not the meaning intended by the Master.

The coming of the Son of Man is the same Christ Birth which the human man Jesus experienced in His earthly time. Each of us holds within us the Christ *seed*, it is our responsibility and indeed our True purpose to prepare the spiritual *soil* that the seed may sprout.

I repeat, this is done only through the inner work of purification of selfhood in cooperation with the Most High. No amount of money paid to any church will work as a substitute, nor any special words spoken.

Many say the name Jesus often, having been misled by blind teachers to believe that in the speaking of this word some magic is done. Some others call out the name Jehovah, thinking it holds some magic power, as if the One Most High God of the Living could have some care of what vernacular was used in reference to Him!

Are we then speaking against prayer here? By no means!

What is here being addressed is the *spirit* in which one prays. What are we praying for? A new car? More money? A promotion or some other station of so called *honor*?

Jesus the Master tells us that our Father knows of all our needs, therefore we must pray in Truth, asking for help in our inner work, asking for understanding of *His* will, forsaking the petty wants of the false self, and forsaking the false self in *knowing* it to *be* false.

When Jesus spoke of doing things in His name, He was speaking from His Most High Christ Self. He was trying to get across to simple people, His message of doing *all* things as an offering to God, through God, in God.

Jesus charges us with the task not of following another *man*, even *himself*, but rather of making the *Way* straight, that the *new* True Man may be born. Jesus was forced to speak in a roundabout way, given the highly superstitious nature of people in his time.

In this day of 2013, people are only slightly more or less superstitious, yet it has been given me to reveal these Truths nonetheless.

Jesus spoke of false Christs to come, and that we should beware of them. Most think this to mean that some man or men will come forth, and claim to *be* Jesus the Christ. This is yet another crippled teaching from the blind. The false Christs which He speaks of are those held up in the churches today being *many*. To date the author has not found a single *Christian* church exempt from this error.

This is why we have thousands of separate churches today all saying something in a different way, yet all claiming possession of the *true* Christ.

The Truth is, no possession dwells in the True Christ, only Absolute Freedom *from* possession.

Jesus gives us clear instructions as to how to proceed. He tells us *what* to look for, as well as *where* to look. What? "Seek Ye *first* the Kingdom of God and His righteousness, and all things will be added to You." Where? "The Kingdom of God is within You."

He encourages us to persevere, to keep trying, if we fall to get up and go on in the True Hope of Christ. This

True Hope is in direct contrast to the false hope of a distant *future* heaven.

Jesus teaches us to turn away from sin.

Our blind teachers tell us of many *sins*, the list seems to grow longer by the day. The Truth is, there is only one sin, that is, the forsaking of our True Source Being One God, call Him by any name you may choose. We have *fallen* into mistaken identity, *thinking* ourselves to be *separate* from our Source which *is* the Lord. Though it is True that we appear as individual entities, we remain One and inseparable *in* the Lord. All of these other so called *sins* are merely outgrowths or outer manifestations of our inner lack of Faith in Truth.

These ignorant acts might be better understood as being *of* sin or full of sin, hence *sinful*. This realization must not be looked upon as a matter of guilt or shame as our churchmen would suggest, but rather as an opportunity to turn away from such ignorance, and error, and instead to turn *towards* the Most High in Truth.

In attempting to fight these so called *sins*, we face an impossible task. This is the reason why so many suffer so much and for so long. We have been misled by blind churchmen (who know no better) to try to quit these *sins*. This is an impossible task, of course, since the *real* sin is overlooked. We must cut the head of the serpent off, instead of wasting time, effort and tears beating its tail.

Jesus further tells us: "None will come to the Father but through Me." Once again, Jesus speaks here from His True Christ Self. He is trying to tell us to give birth, or give *Way* to this True Christ Self, the True *Me* within each of us.

We may call upon the name of Jesus to eternity without one step of progress in Truth. Only in the *realization* of one's own True Christ Self will one find the *Way* to the Father. And again, this may only be accomplished through the shedding of the false self, called by Jesus, *Satan*.

We often hear it said popularly: "Believe in yourself." This is of no value to those which do not yet *know* who they are in Truth!

When we try to change ourselves, we fail at every attempt. What is needed is not the changing of the false self, as this will inevitably circle back to bring us further suffering. What is needed is the realization of the True Self *within*. This True Self cannot be changed, as it is the very inflowing of the One Most High God.

The Truth is revealed only when all which is false is discarded and abandoned.

JESUS THE MAN

Jesus lived and died working to show men the Way to True Freedom from the chains of religion. He went through great trials for His Work in showing people True Faith, as opposed to mere religious belief.

Men have reduced this Great Life of Jesus to a mockery. This is the reason why most common people today will run away from the mere mention of His name. Others (out of fear) engage in a form of mental idol worship, imagining Jesus coming to the rescue, *through the clouds.*

NOTE (*Let the reader know that the clouds here spoken of in the revealed scripture, means* WORDS). The revelation being beyond mere words, in Spirit and in Truth.

These idol worshippers, known to the world as *the faithful,* are held suspended from True Spiritual progress by their own fearful false self-created hell. They have been reduced to idle *waiters,* seeing themselves as helpless victims, weeping and indulging in self-pity, and self-deception.

Let it be known that the purpose of this book is not the founding of a new religion. The author is not attempting to gather followers. The aim is to help those who have eyes and ears to find their own *Way*, to give up being *followers*.

I am not asking anyone to believe me, nor to believe *in* me, as either of these would be grave errors.

What I am asking, is for the reader to open his or her mind and heart to the Absolute Truth, apprehended directly at the Supreme Source *of* Truth, the Living God with Us.

What follows in the next section of this work is a crude framework of an imperfect discipline. This discipline has been developed through much study of a vast expanse of teachings and scriptures, and has taken many years to put down on paper. It is imperfect in that so is its author.

If you, as you are reading these words are Truly Free and Joyful in your Heart and Mind, then you have no need of this book or of the teaching of the discipline which follows.

If however, you do not find yourself Free and Joyful, or if you feel a nagging dark presence is keeping you from Freedom, I beg you to read on.

The Master bids us: "Seek, and Ye shall find." Then goes on to tell where to look: "The Kingdom of God is within You." (It's worth repeating.)

Before this *finding* can be done, however, the secret inner place must be made empty, empty of ideas and belief systems of others, these are 99 percent distractions or mental idols. The secret place must be made empty of self-hood, as is stated in the early text of Luke as quoted by Meister Eckhart.

Luke 14:26 (as it appears today):

"If anyone comes to Me and does not hate his father and mother, wife and children, brothers and sisters, yes, and his own life also, he cannot be My disciple."

Jesus teaching us to hate? I don't believe it!

Luke 14:26 (as it appeared in the time of Meister Eckhart, 13th century A.D.):

"Who does not abandon his selfhood, cannot be My disciple."

A child can see the stark difference, and the purpose in the storytellers making the change.

I beg you to read on, find the Truth in its Perfect State, with no influence of men.

I assure you, the Book of Life is *not* the Bible nor is it any other book of mere words. Do the work, daily, hourly, moment by moment, in all things you think, speak and do, be True. Have Faith in the Truth!

Do not despair, keep on the *Way* and you will drop the walking death that has masqueraded as Life.

You will know what it Truly means to Live.

You will no longer struggle because "Being perfect *is* a struggle."

Perfect Being is *the* Gift.

PART TWO

The *Way* of Perfection for the Imperfect

It could be said that there is no darkness, only absence of light. Upon closer observation we might say that light is never absent, only prevented entry. Light, by its very nature will enter instantly any place which offers an opening. It may be more to the point to say: The Absolute Law which governs all things, including light, allows that light will enter instantly any place which offers an opening.

One cannot touch light, yet we don't deny it's *Being*. Spirit falls into this same class of Being, and is likewise governed by the Absolute Law.

IMPORTANT TO NOTE: The Light or Spirit here spoken of comes from Within, hence from Above.

Spirit and the discipline required to foster its entry into One's realization is our topic.

Rationally speaking, the first step in this process would seem to be the definition of Spirit.

Let us begin by saying that Spirit is the underlying root essence of a given principle, be it virtuous or pernicious. This leads us to the next logical question: "What Spiritual Principle do we wish to investigate? The answer being: We want to investigate the Highest Principle, therefore the Highest Spirit.

ABSOLUTE TRUTH

That that is presented as the *truth* which is not upheld by the inner Absolute Truth may be rightly called "propaganda." The imposter self is often manifested as propaganda both internally and externally.

Internal propaganda may be compared with the mental dialog, this is the false voice of the imposter self-assuring us that what we are thinking, saying or doing is right or at least *justified*. This is also often propped up with thoughts such as "I have no choice." The imposters' sole priority is ever its own survival.

External propaganda is found within nations, clubs, religions, political parties, companies and even families. This propaganda may be manifested as pledges, dogmas, fear campaigns and many other group belief systems and devices.

The most effective form of propaganda is upheld, protected and propagated by its victim, or victims.

The Absolute Truth may not be learned by the reading and memorization of the written word, regardless how holy we may think the book. It may not be learned by listening to speeches or preachings by any woman or man, regardless of how holy we may think them. The Absolute Truth may not be obtained through suffering, or what is commonly known as "self-sacrifice." It may not be obtained by the practice of many rituals or chants, regardless of how holy or magic we may think them.

Absolute Truth may not be obtained through belief systems or the faith in them, regardless how holy we may think them or how many believers join in the systems.

The Spirit of Absolute Truth by Law may not enter the sacred inner place of one's realization unless that place first be made pure. The purity we speak of is not a religious ideal. It is rather an ongoing work that must be taken on by each who desires the direct apprehension of this Truth.

The Imposter Self

The first step in this ongoing work is the identification of what it is which is occupying the sacred inner place. We may call this obstruction within, the imposter self. This is the false and petty self, which we have built up through the thinking mind, and through the thinking mind it may be dismantled.

It must here be understood, however, that the thinking mind must only be used as a tool in order that we may know the place in which to find freedom from the imposter self. This place may be called the present moment, or the *Now*.

It may seem strange to the reader to look at the present moment or the *Now* as a place rather than a time. This strangeness is born of the Truth that the *Now* is out of time, this is stated that the reader may know that this Freedom from the imposter cannot be found in time.

This *Now* spoken of must not be confused with any of the objects which may be experienced in the moment, but it is rather the pure moment itself, empty of all objects. Objects in this sense could be possessions, thoughts, ideas, one's company or even one's circumstances or health.

As long as we remain under the spell of the imposter self, in Truth we are not awake, or conscious in any moment. In order to dissolve this spell we must develop through discipline what may be called conscious presence. I beg the reader to understand the word *spell* here used is not intended to suggest some superstitious notion of evil spirits, but no other word in our language captures the power here spoken of. This power is psychic and may only be dissolved through conscious presence. Of this more will be said later in this work.

The imposter offers us a view of life screened through its belief systems and fear based strategies, and assures us that no other life exists. As we observe the imposter we become aware that it is the Observer who is real and True. This practised observation gradually weakens the hypnotic effect of the imposter. With continued practice, we begin to glimpse the True Life *directly*, and to realize it as a reflection of what we *are* in Truth.

It is very important to take care not to resist or try to fight or defeat this imposter self. Simply hold your awareness on this imposter whenever you may feel it is interfering. Telltale signs which alert us of the imposters' interference may manifest as, anger, jealousy, rage, indulgent giddy happiness or its opposite, indulgent sadness or depression. Fear, anxiety and self-pity also often suggest imposter interference.

This imposter is only real to the extent which we think it real, through self-deception.

When first we begin this work, the imposter may resist strongly, this is to be anticipated by the worker. When the imposters' resistance is felt we know that we have dealt it a blow through the light of our conscious attention. At such times when we feel that we are sad, for example, it is often helpful to ask the question "Who is sad?" This simple practice brings the worker Home to the Truth.

The imposter manifests itself in two ways, the first and seemingly most important to each of us is the individual aspect. The second aspect is the collective imposter self, which is created, strengthened and maintained by the interaction and most often conflict between individual imposter selves.

Examples of potential collective imposter selves are, nations, religions, political parties and many other belief sharing group systems.

This is not to say that being part of any of these clubs, groups or churches is *necessarily* harmful. The disease occurs only when we look for our identity *in* or *through* the group, and/or its systems of belief or ideology. It is enough to say that there is the *potential* for self-deception and identity confusion if one is not aware of the *possibility* of falling into such traps.

We must be mindful also of the trap which is that of trying to change the world. It is in the True realization that we each create our world as a reflection of our own dominant inner selves, that we may see that the one and only way to change the world is to See to it through Self-discipline that our dominant inner Self is not the imposter self. This is what is meant by *purification*. Many spend the greater portion of their adult lives trying to change themselves, this is time and energy wasted. All that is needed is the discovery or realization of the True Self, empty of the imposter.

It is critical to note the importance of the view of the Light of Absolute Truth as entering from within, or rather the realization that it has always been within us unseen and obscured by the interference of the imposter self.

Conscious Presence

Continuously introducing ourselves to things, circumstances and our Company (directly) without mental commentary or judgement, taking in all just as it is free of future expectation and past regret, we develop at first a habit of presence and consciousness gradually taking place of the former habit of absence and unconsciousness. Through sustained attention to such discipline, presence and consciousness become the dominant state, bringing about the awakening of One's True Nature.

Such awakening should be viewed as a verb inasmuch as it is a continual Work, so to speak. Seen in this light, it becomes clear that no end appears to exist either in the Work or in the Worker.

ABSOLUTE TRUTH
LEADS TO ABSOLUTE FREEDOM

The discipline previously outlined is not intended to be a hobby, nor a Sunday distraction.

If the reader is True in his or her commitment to Freedom and to the Absolute Truth, then this discipline will be looked upon as a *Way* of Life.

I must caution the reader on two very important points.

First, as you practice this discipline you will encounter moments of great clarity, this is fine and may be exhilarating. keep your balance, remain even minded, avoid extreme highs or lows. Also, avoid the trap of thinking you've *made it*. Keep it ever foremost in mind that this is an ongoing awakening process.

There is no end zone!

Secondly, and of equal importance, avoid trying to convince others of what you've experienced. What you are realizing is your True Self, and this is specially made for you alone. Only if someone asks you directly for advice will you want to give it, and then it should be seasoned with the idea that each must find his or her own *Way*.

I must mention again the important technique that may be used daily, hourly and even at times moment by moment. Whenever we feel the interference of the imposter self, easily recognized by negative and destructive moods or emotions such as anger, jealousy, fear, resentment, envy, hatred or anxiety, we must step back and ask "Who is feeling this?" Since we know that the True Highest Self cannot be touched by such as these, we presently *see* the Truth, that these feelings or emotions are the property of the imposter, and therefore must be abandoned.

We should also apply this technique when we notice self-pity at work or giddy happiness or its opposite, dark depression and doubt. Know that True happiness and joy are well and good, the giddy happiness above spoken of is of a different nature, it is indulgent and reveals itself as escapism, self-deception and distraction.

Remember, do not fall into the trap of resisting the imposter self. Simply *look* at the Truth that these negative emotions are not *Me*. When we resist the imposter, or attempt to fight it, we somehow give it power, and may get carried away in old negative thought habits.

As we bring ourselves back Home to the Truth using these tools, over time these negative emotions and thought habits will wither and fall away.

I promise you, if you stick with this discipline, and remain starkly honest with yourself, working in cooperation with the Most High, you will find your *Way*.

At last you will be Truly Alive!

PEACE AND QUIET
BOTH INNER AND OUTER

Something should be said with regard to the general atmosphere or climate of one's mental state. In the practice of the discipline here spoken of, one's state of mind will become more still, more tranquil, more open. In light of this, we may find it helpful to seek out when possible, an outer atmosphere of calmness and quiet. Certainly this will not be possible at all times, especially for those with busy careers and household/family duties. Still, if we are sincere in our desire for the *High Way*, we will make time, so to speak, for some quiet reflective periods in which to sort the desirable from the undesirable qualities of mind.

I hesitate to call this reflectiveness "meditation," simply because of the preconceived ideas and prejudices held by so many in the west. Most of this prejudice and fear is generated by a propaganda of ignorance, originating in the popular churches, popular culture and a slanted media view.

This fear is rooted in ignorance and misunderstanding. I have spoken with many who have a great fear that they may become lost in some sort of a superstitious trance if they dared to sit in meditation. Meditation practised correctly is in no way an escape from reality, as many misunderstand it to be. In fact, it could be better described as an escape from fantasy and denial. The majority of the population spend most, if not all of their lives in a daydream of sorts, imagining how things could or should be. This is due to the mistaken idea or belief system which tells us that our inner peace is dependent upon outer circumstances. Many believe their discontent to be caused by their pain and disease or circumstance, when in Truth just the reverse is the case. Though it is true that one cannot deny the relative reality of outer temporary circumstances, still, we must bear in mind the Knowledge that True permanent Peace comes from within our True Highest Being.

Many others fear meditation because they connect it with Buddha or Krishna, thinking that Jesus or Jehovah would be angry with them for worshipping a *false god*, never grasping the Truth that the One True God is called by many names.

As we sit in a state of quiet reflectiveness, we will *see* thoughts passing by. Excessive thinking has become a negative habit. We believe that we must give great importance to our every thought, and we have come to think that our thoughts are who we Truly *are*.

This is an error.

Thoughts are simply thoughts, passing and with no lasting Being of their own. We need not fight them, simply watch them pass, and in this act we know that as the *Watcher*, we are *not* the thoughts.

Often we will hear people or ourselves say "I don't have time for..." This opening line is often followed by words such as: quiet time, meditation, relaxation or even rest. This is only true if we will it to be so.

Many people will structure their lives so as not to have a moment in the day free of distraction and activity. All too often this is done because of past experiences with moments of stillness in which we looked at ourselves briefly, didn't like what we saw, so we ran away into further distraction and denial. This obsessive *busy-ness* may also stem from the old churchman lie (with no True scriptural basis) which says: "Idle hands are the Devil's workshop." This lie was put into place to keep the population firmly in the yoke of psycho-economic slavery. In this way the slave masters have saved much whip leather, as their underlings mentally whip themselves into servitude in fear of death and of course, *Hell's fire*.

A wise man once said: "The gates of Hell are locked from the inside."

These so-called "slave masters" must also be forgiven; however, if we are to be True followers of the *Way* as taught by the Master Jesus. In their crippled and blinded condition they fail to *see* that they also are enslaved in this culture of ignorance and self-deception. In the Master's words: "Forgive them Father, for they know not what they do."

Freedom is a choice, it may not be granted or taken away except by One's own volition.

Each and every one of us holds his or her own keys to Absolute Freedom. We have lost sight of this Truth through the false belief systems which instruct us to look outside, and to others for our Freedom.

True Freedom is *lived* fearlessly *in* the One Lord Being Truth.

If after reading these last few lines, you find yourself saying to yourself: "Yeah butt..."

Then you are in need of this practice most of all.

I will not wish you *luck*.

You have no need of it!